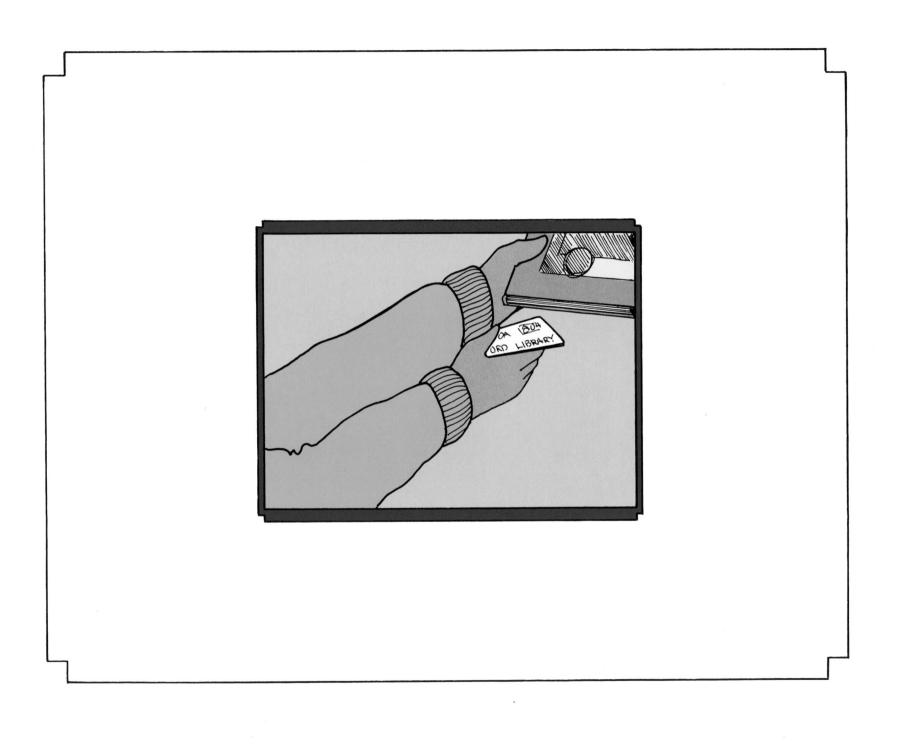

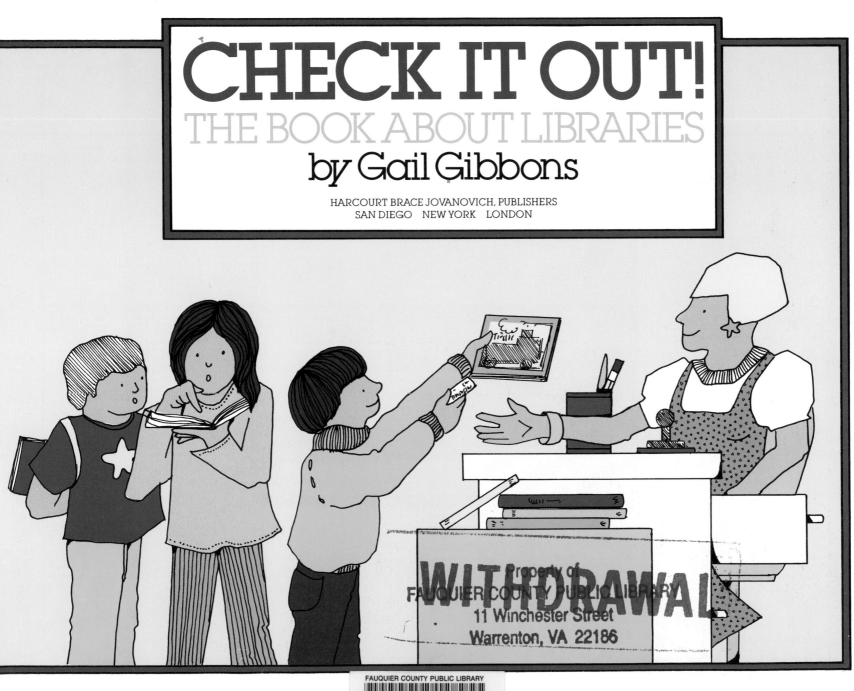

CHECK IT OUT!
THE BOOK ABOUT LIBRARIES
by Gail Gibbons

HARCOURT BRACE JOVANOVICH, PUBLISHERS
SAN DIEGO NEW YORK LONDON

For my friend Caroline Ward

Requests for permission to make copies of any part of the work should be mailed to: Permissions Department, Harcourt Brace Jovanovich, Publishers, 8th Floor, Orlando, Florida 32887.

Library of Congress Cataloging in Publication Data

Gibbons, Gail.
Check it out!

Summary: Discusses what is found in a library and how different libraries serve their communities.
1. Libraries—Juvenile literature. [1. Libraries]
I. Title.
ISBN 0-15-216400-6
ISBN 0-15-216401-4 (pbk.)

Printed and bound by South China Printing Co. Ltd., Hong Kong
D E F G H
B C D E F (pbk.)

Special thanks to Marianne Cassell of the Vermont Department of Libraries, Montpelier, Vermont; Patty Eckles of the Howe Library, Hanover, New Hampshire; and Margaret Drew and Doris Honig of the Bradford Public Library, Bradford, Vermont.

HBJ

There are small libraries . . .

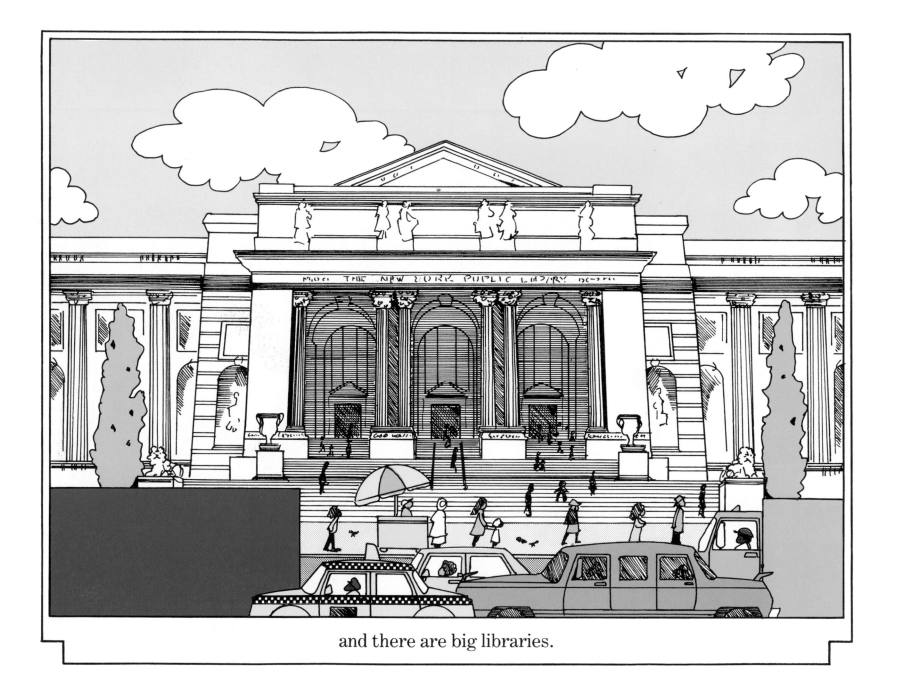

and there are big libraries.

The biggest library in the United States is the Library of Congress in Washington, D.C. Most books published in this country are kept there— millions and millions of books.

No matter what its size, a library is filled with books and information. The word *library* comes from the Latin word for book—*liber*.

Before there were books, words were written on tablets of clay or on scrolls.
Later, medieval monks lettered whole books by hand, which took a long time.

Now libraries have printed books. Modern printing presses print thousands of books in a short time.

There are different kinds of libraries. Public libraries . . .

and school libraries have books and information about everything
you need to know.

Other libraries have special collections of books.

There are all kinds of books in a library.

Finding the book you want takes practice. Libraries are organized in different ways. If you are looking for a particular book, you can ask a librarian to help you . . .

The call number is the "address" for the book. It helps the reader to find the book on the shelf.

call number

author card

Gibbons, Gail.
    Sun up, sun down / written and
illustrated by Gail Gibbons. -- San
Diego : Harcourt Brace Jovanovich,
c1983.
    p. cm.
    Summary: Describes the
characteristics of the sun and the ways
in which it regulates life on earth.
    ISBN 0-15-282781-1

    1. Sun--Pictorial works--Juvenile
literature. I. Title

23 NOV 83 MARG   VSNKdc   82-23420

title card

Sun up, sun down
J
523.7

Gibbons, Gail.
    Sun up, sun down / written and
illustrated by Gail Gibbons. -- San
Diego : Harcourt Brace Jovanovich,
c1983.
    p. cm.
    Summary: Describes the
characteristics of the sun and the ways
in which it regulates life on earth.
    ISBN 0-15-282781-1

    1. Sun--Pictorial works--Juvenile
literature. I. Title

23 NOV 83 MARG   VSNKdc   82-23420

subject card

SUN--PICTORIAL WORKS--JUVENILE
LITERATURE.
J
523.7

Gibbons, Gail.
    Sun up, sun down / written and
illustrated by Gail Gibbons. -- San
Diego : Harcourt Brace Jovanovich,
c1983.
    p. cm.
    Summary: Describes the
characteristics of the sun and the ways
in which it regulates life on earth.
    ISBN 0-15-282781-1

    1. Sun--Pictorial works--Juvenile
literature. I. Title

23 NOV 83 MARG   VSNKdc   82-23420

LA–LF   LG–LZ   M   M–NI

PO–PZ   Q   SI–SU

V   W–WO   Y   Z

or you can use the card catalog . . .

a book catalog, or a computer.

A book can be read at the library . . .

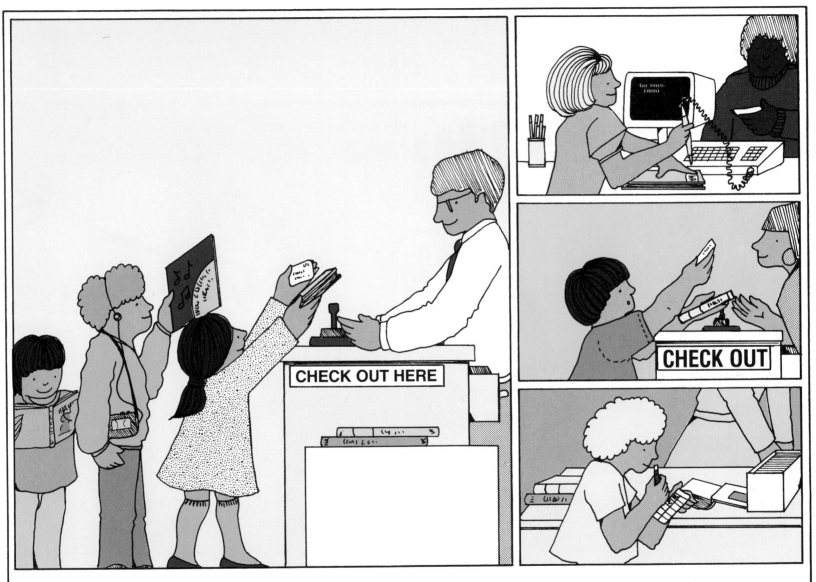

or it can be checked out and taken home. To keep track of who has the books, libraries use either a computer, a library card, or sometimes just a signature.

When books are returned, they are checked in and placed back on the shelves for other people to read. If a book is not returned on time, or if a book is damaged, the library usually charges the reader a fine.

Librarians are always ready to help you find a good book to read, and they are available to answer questions, even over the phone.

Librarians acquire books and information from various sources. They select materials by reading reviews, listening to suggestions, going to meetings, and looking at catalogs. Librarians must follow a budget. Most of the money in a library budget comes from taxes.

Sometimes people donate books to the library. Some people donate their time, volunteering to help with tasks that keep the library running smoothly. Many libraries have groups called Friends of the Library, who assist the library with special projects, such as raising funds.

Public libraries and school libraries have different sections for different age groups.

Libraries also have special books, services, and equipment for the handicapped.

Libraries will sometimes deliver books to people who cannot get to the library building. In some areas, bookmobiles, which are libraries on wheels, visit people who don't have a library nearby.

Besides books, the library contains records and tapes, computers . . .

puzzles and toys, microfilm equipment, newspapers and magazines . . .

reference books, maps, globes, and much more.

Many activities take place at the library. There may be puppet shows, movies, story hours, summer reading programs, and arts and crafts classes.

Often there are special exhibits. Authors and artists may come to the library to talk about their work.

The library is the perfect place to learn about new things, to find the answers to questions, and most important, to enjoy the fun of reading!